AN INTRODUCTION TO ENGLISH LITERATURE

A COMPREHENSIVE GUIDE

MR. D. PRADEEK, MS. J. MERCY RANI, MS. S. RUFINA ROSLIN MARY

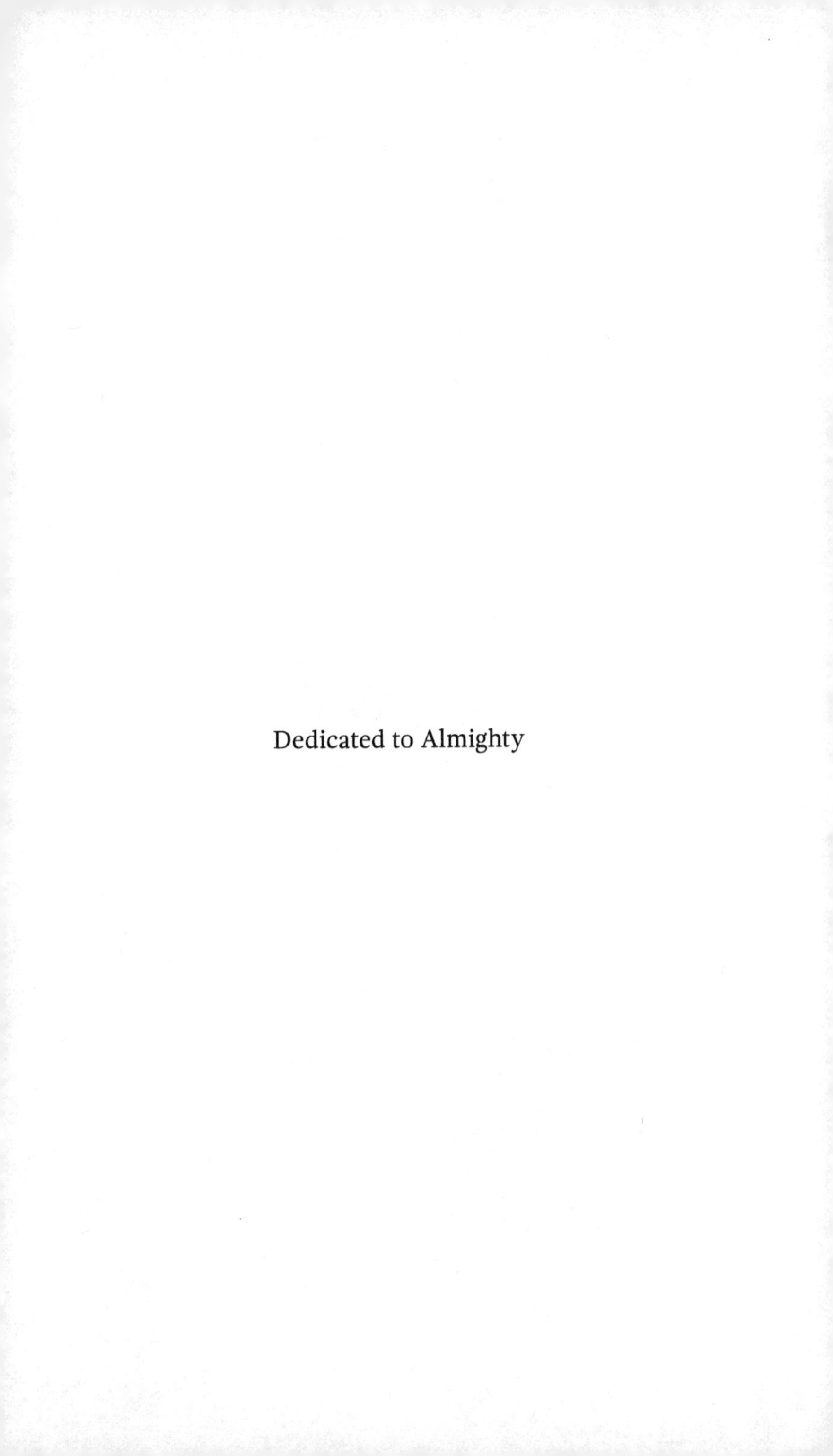

Dedicated to Almighty

Contents

Foreword

English literature, with its rich tapestry of stories, poems, and plays, offers an intricate reflection of the human experience. From the earliest Old English texts to the contemporary works that shape our world today, literature has been the lens through which we examine society, explore the complexities of the human soul, and record our history. In An Introduction to English Literature: A Comprehensive Guide, we embark on a journey that traces this evolution, from its humble beginnings to its profound impact on modern thought.

This book serves as both a starting point and a companion for those venturing into the vast and ever-evolving world of English literature. Whether you are a student just beginning to explore the subject, an enthusiast seeking deeper understanding, or someone simply wishing to reconnect with the classics, this guide provides clarity and context to make the study of literature both accessible and enriching.

Within these pages, you will find not only the analysis of individual works and authors but also a broader exploration of literary movements, historical contexts, and thematic threads that connect the diverse spectrum of English writing. The goal is not just to understand the words on the page, but to engage with them, to question them, and to see how they reflect and challenge the world we live in.

By offering a structured approach to the study of literature, this guide ensures that readers come away with a comprehensive understanding of the key texts, authors, and concepts that have shaped the English literary tradition. Through this understanding, we hope to foster a deeper appreciation for the power of words and the enduring relevance of literature in our lives.

May this guide inspire you to read with curiosity, reflect with insight, and engage with English literature in a way that transforms both your understanding of the written word and the world around you.

Welcome to the world of English literature. Enjoy the journey.

CHAPTER I

Introduction to English Literature

English literature is a vast, diverse, and evolving field that spans over a thousand years, capturing human experiences, emotions, and ideas through written works in the English language. It encompasses a range of genres, themes, and styles, reflecting the social, cultural, and political shifts of each historical period. From epic poetry and classic plays to novels and contemporary experimental writing, English literature has continually transformed to address the issues and concerns of its time.

What is English Literature?

English literature refers to works written in the English language by authors from various parts of the world, including England, the United States, Canada, Australia, and many other regions. It is distinguished by its linguistic variety, rich storytelling, and its ability to mirror and critique human society. It includes not only fiction—like novels, plays, and poetry—but also non-fiction works, such as essays, autobiographies, and speeches that have contributed significantly to intellectual and cultural life.

Why Study English Literature?

Studying English literature opens a window into different cultures, philosophies, and historical events. Literature serves as both a reflection and a critique of society, providing insights into the minds and motivations of people across time periods and social classes. It helps readers develop critical thinking, empathy, and a deeper understanding of the complexities of human nature. By engaging with literary analysis, readers learn to examine not just the narrative but also the underlying themes, symbols, and intentions that enrich the text.

Key Genres in English Literature

English literature comprises multiple genres, each with its own conventions and purposes:

1. **Poetry** - A condensed, often rhythmic form of writing that uses language and form to evoke emotions. Key poetic forms include sonnets, ballads, haikus, and free verse.
2. **Drama** - A genre intended for performance, including tragedy, comedy, and tragicomedy. Drama explores characters, dialogues, and conflicts that are often societal or internal, making it deeply relatable and impactful.
3. **Fiction** - Primarily novels and short stories that present imagined events and characters. This genre offers vast creative freedom, allowing for a rich exploration of themes, settings, and human experiences.
4. **Non-Fiction** - Essays, autobiographies, and biographies that provide factual or personal perspectives on events, people, and concepts.
5. **The Novel** - One of the most prominent genres in English literature, novels allow for complex character development and the exploration of broad themes over an extended narrative.

Major Historical Movements in English Literature

Throughout history, English literature has been shaped by cultural, political, and intellectual changes. Key periods include:

1. **Old English and Medieval Periods (450–1500)**
   Early English literature began with epic poetry, like *Beowulf*, which was rooted in oral tradition and centered on themes of heroism, honor, and fate. Medieval literature, such as Geoffrey Chaucer's *The Canterbury Tales*, started exploring diverse characters and social commentary.

2. **The Renaissance (1500–1660)**
   This period witnessed a revival of classical learning and a flowering of creativity in England, with an emphasis on humanism, individualism, and secularism. William Shakespeare, Christopher Marlowe, and John Milton are notable writers from this era. Shakespeare's plays, exploring human nature and societal issues, are central to this period.

3. **The Enlightenment and 18th Century (1660–1780)**
   Literature in this period focused on reason, science, and satire. Writers like Jonathan Swift and Alexander Pope used wit and satire to critique societal norms. The early novel also emerged, with Daniel Defoe's *Robinson Crusoe* and Samuel Richardson's *Pamela* signaling a new literary form.

4. **The Romantic Period (1780–1832)**
   Romanticism reacted against Enlightenment values by emphasizing emotion, nature, and individualism. Poets like William Wordsworth, John Keats, and Percy Bysshe Shelley celebrated the power of imagination and nature's beauty.

5. **The Victorian Era (1832–1901)**
   Marked by industrialization and social change, Victorian literature often addressed social issues, morality, and class. Charles Dickens, Charlotte Brontë, and Thomas Hardy captured the complexities of Victorian society,

while authors like Oscar Wilde and George Eliot explored human psychology.

6. **The Modernist Period (1901–1945)**
Modernist writers broke traditional narrative forms and experimented with stream-of-consciousness, fragmented structure, and complex symbolism. Influential figures like Virginia Woolf, James Joyce, and T.S. Eliot focused on themes of alienation, disillusionment, and the inner workings of the mind.

7. **Postmodernism and Contemporary Literature (1945–Present)**
Postmodernism challenges conventions and embraces irony, pastiche, and paradox. Authors like Salman Rushdie, Margaret Atwood, and Don DeLillo blur the line between reality and fiction, often questioning the nature of truth and identity. Contemporary literature also reflects multiculturalism and global perspectives.

Introduction to Literary Analysis
Literary analysis is the practice of examining a text's structure, themes, language, and meaning. It involves:

1. **Understanding Theme and Motif** - Identifying the central messages or ideas in a work, and how these are expressed through recurring images or concepts.
2. **Character Analysis** - Examining the personalities, motivations, and relationships of characters, understanding how they contribute to the story and its themes.
3. **Symbolism** - Recognizing objects, colors, or images that represent larger ideas or concepts, adding depth to the narrative.

4. **Tone and Mood** - Analyzing the author's attitude (tone) and the emotional atmosphere (mood) created for the reader.
5. **Form and Structure** - Observing how the organization of a text, its sentence structure, and stylistic choices enhance the narrative or thematic elements.
6. **Historical and Cultural Context** - Understanding the time and place in which a text was written, which can provide insight into its themes, characters, and plot.

English literature is not merely a collection of stories but a window into the human condition. It reflects the values, struggles, and dreams of different eras, continually evolving to explore new themes and perspectives. By studying literature, we gain a greater understanding of humanity's shared experiences, from ancient epics to modern novels, making English literature a timeless and essential field of study.

CHAPTER II

Old English Literature (450–1150): The Roots of English Literature

Old English literature, also known as Anglo-Saxon literature, marks the earliest phase of English literary tradition. Written in Old English, a language vastly different from modern English, this period's works reflect the values, beliefs, and culture of early medieval England, especially the themes of heroism, loyalty, fate, and the interplay between pagan and Christian elements.

Historical Context

The Old English period began with the arrival of the Anglo-Saxons in Britain around the 5th century, following the Roman withdrawal. These tribes brought their Germanic language and culture, which would later evolve into Old English. The early Anglo-Saxon society was tribal, with loyalty to leaders and kin playing a central role. However, with the spread of Christianity from the 7th century onward, pagan traditions began to blend with Christian values, creating a unique cultural and literary fusion.

Key Characteristics of Old English Literature

Old English literature primarily consisted of oral poetry, which was later transcribed into manuscripts by monks. It was characterized by the following features:

1. **Alliterative Verse**: Old English poetry often used alliteration, or the repetition of initial consonant sounds, as a structural device. Rather than relying on rhyme, poems were constructed with alliteration to create rhythm and cohesion within each line.

2. **Kennings**: Kennings were compound expressions used in place of simple nouns. For example, the sea was often called the "whale-road" (hwæl-weġ), and the sun might be referred to as the "sky-candle." These metaphorical expressions enriched the language and gave depth to simple ideas.

3. **Themes of Heroism and Loyalty**: Many Old English works celebrated heroic deeds, loyalty to one's lord, and the warrior code, as in the epic *Beowulf*. The warrior culture of the Anglo-Saxons placed great value on courage, strength, and loyalty to one's leader, which often provided the backbone of these tales.

4. **Blend of Pagan and Christian Elements**: While Anglo-Saxon society was initially pagan, the influence of Christianity introduced themes of faith, divine providence, and morality. This blend can be seen in works where Christian and pagan ideals coexist, reflecting the cultural shift of the time.

5. **Elegiac Tone**: Many Old English poems express a sense of loss or lament, possibly influenced by the harsh realities of life during this period, including war, disease, and political instability. Elegies such as *The Wanderer* and *The Seafarer* reflect themes of exile, isolation, and yearning for a lost past.

Major Works and Themes

1. Beowulf

Beowulf is the most famous and enduring work of Old English literature, an epic poem of over 3,000 lines. It tells the story of Beowulf, a heroic warrior from Geatland, who comes to aid the Danish king Hrothgar by defeating the monster Grendel. Later, Beowulf also confronts Grendel's vengeful mother and, in his final act, a dragon that threatens his homeland.

The themes in *Beowulf* include bravery, the heroic code, loyalty to one's lord, and the inevitability of death. Although it includes pagan elements like fate (wyrd) and legendary monsters, Christian values and allusions are also present, showing the period's cultural transition.

2. The Wanderer

An elegy, *The Wanderer* is a poem of 115 lines that expresses themes of exile, isolation, and nostalgia for lost times. It tells the story of a man who has lost his lord and comrades and is left to wander alone. As he reflects on his loneliness, he also meditates on the transience of life and the futility of earthly pursuits, a theme that aligns with Christian ideals of humility and spiritual endurance.

3. The Seafarer

Similar in tone to *The Wanderer*, *The Seafarer* also explores themes of exile and the hardships of life. This poem combines pagan and Christian elements as the speaker meditates on the trials of life at sea, contrasting the suffering and isolation of physical existence with the hope of salvation and the eternal life promised by Christianity.

4. The Dream of the Rood

One of the most remarkable Old English religious poems, *The Dream of the Rood* presents a unique perspective on the crucifixion of Christ. Written from the viewpoint of the cross (or "rood") itself, the poem depicts Christ as a heroic warrior who willingly sacrifices himself. This work combines Christian teachings with the heroic ethos familiar to the Anglo-Saxons, presenting Jesus as a leader who meets death with courage and strength.

Cultural and Religious Significance

Old English literature is notable for its portrayal of both pagan and Christian values, reflecting the cultural synthesis occurring in Anglo-Saxon England. Pagan values, such as the warrior code and loyalty to one's lord, coexist with Christian teachings on faith, humility, and salvation. This duality is visible in many Old English texts, which often praise courage and honor while also promoting Christian ideals of forgiveness and the hope for eternal life.

Additionally, Old English poetry often reflects a society deeply connected to the natural world. Many poems evoke vivid images of landscapes, seas, and storms, illustrating the close relationship between people and their environment, which was crucial for survival in this period.

Literary Legacy

The Old English period laid the foundation for English literature by developing themes and narrative techniques that would recur in later works. The heroic values, use of metaphor, and blending of belief systems seen in Old English works like *Beowulf* and *The Wanderer* influenced subsequent literature, from medieval romances to modern epics. Old English literature also provides historical insights into Anglo-Saxon society, including its values, beliefs, and challenges, serving as a vital record of early English cultural identity.

Old English literature marks the beginning of English literary history, embodying the themes, values, and artistry of a society transitioning from pagan traditions to Christian beliefs. Its alliterative verse, use of kennings, and blend of heroism with spiritual reflection continue to captivate readers, providing a glimpse into the foundations of English storytelling. The Old English period reminds us that the struggles and triumphs of humanity are timeless, resonating across centuries in themes of courage, loyalty, loss, and faith.

CHAPTER III

Middle English Literature (1150–1500): From Chaucer to Malory

The Middle English period marked a significant transformation in English literature. Spanning from the Norman Conquest to the late 15th century, this era saw the development of a distinctly English literary identity that emerged from the blend of Anglo-Saxon, Norman, and French influences. The language evolved from Old English to Middle English, making literature more accessible to the growing number of English-speaking people. This period produced some of the most celebrated works in English literary history, including the writings of Geoffrey Chaucer, the mystical works of Julian of Norwich, and the chivalric tales of Sir Thomas Malory.

Historical and Cultural Context

The Middle English period began after the Norman Conquest of 1066, which brought profound social, political, and linguistic changes to England. Norman French became the language of the ruling class, while Latin was used in religious and scholarly contexts, leaving Old English in decline. Over time, however, a new form of English emerged from this linguistic mix, resulting in what we now call Middle English. By the 14th century, English had reasserted itself, becoming the language of literature, government, and common life.

The period was marked by feudalism, chivalry, and the influence of the Church. The Crusades and the Hundred Years' War introduced new cultural and literary influences. With a rising sense of national identity, literature in Middle English became a means for exploring social, religious, and ethical themes, paving the way for a more secular and diverse literary culture.

Major Literary Themes and Characteristics

Middle English literature reflects the complexities of a society navigating shifting identities, moral concerns, and religious devotion. Key themes include:

1. **Courtly Love and Chivalry**: Inspired by French romances, tales of chivalry, valor, and courtly love were popular. They celebrated ideals of knightly honor and often involved quests, battles, and romance, as seen in Arthurian legends and tales of knighthood.

2. **Religious Devotion and Morality**: Religion remained central to life, and many Middle English texts are devotional or didactic, aiming to instruct readers in Christian values. This era produced a wealth of spiritual writing, from mystical visions to moral allegories like *Piers Plowman*.

3. **Social Satire and Commentary**: As English literature diversified, writers began to critique social institutions, including the Church and feudal system. Chaucer's *The Canterbury Tales* is a prime example, using humor and satire to explore class distinctions and moral hypocrisies.

4. **Allegory**: Many Middle English works are allegorical, using symbolic characters and narratives to explore

ethical and spiritual themes. Allegory provided a means for writers to address complex ideas about human nature, sin, and salvation.

Key Works and Authors

1. *The Canterbury Tales* by Geoffrey Chaucer

Geoffrey Chaucer (c. 1343–1400) is often called the "Father of English Literature." His masterpiece, *The Canterbury Tales*, is a collection of stories told by a diverse group of pilgrims traveling to the shrine of Thomas Becket in Canterbury. Through characters from different social backgrounds—a knight, a miller, a pardoner, a prioress, and others—Chaucer paints a vivid picture of 14th-century England and satirizes the behaviors, beliefs, and hypocrisies of society. The tales include various genres—romance, fabliaux (comic tales), and moral stories—showcasing Chaucer's versatility and his pioneering use of Middle English in a way that was accessible to many readers.

2. *Piers Plowman* by William Langland

Written by William Langland in the late 14th century, *Piers Plowman* is an allegorical narrative poem that explores the search for a true Christian life. The protagonist, Will, encounters a variety of allegorical figures representing virtues and vices as he journeys toward spiritual fulfillment. *Piers Plowman* critiques the corruption of the Church and society, reflecting the era's concern with morality and social justice. Its themes of charity, honesty, and faith made it one of the most significant religious and social commentaries of the time.

3. *Sir Gawain and the Green Knight*

This anonymous chivalric romance, written in the late 14th century, tells the story of Sir Gawain, a knight of King Arthur's Round Table, and his encounter with the mysterious Green Knight. This tale combines elements of adventure, bravery, and courtly love with a deep exploration of human flaws and moral integrity. Sir Gawain's journey reflects the ideals of chivalry while testing the limits of human virtue and the nature of honor.

4. *Revelations of Divine Love* byJulian of Norwich

Julian of Norwich (c. 1342–1416) was a mystic and anchoress who wrote *Revelations of Divine Love*, the first known book written in English by a woman. Her work is an account of a series of visions she experienced during an illness, offering profound reflections on the nature of God's love, suffering, and salvation. Her optimistic view of divine compassion and the idea that "all shall be well" have made her a beloved figure in Christian literature.

5. *Le Morte d'Arthur* bySir Thomas Malory

Written by Sir Thomas Malory in the 15th century, *Le Morte d'Arthur* is a collection of Arthurian legends that became the definitive English account of King Arthur and his knights. Malory compiled various tales, adding his interpretation of themes like chivalry, loyalty, and betrayal. The work captures the idealism of the Arthurian code while also presenting a tragic view of human nature, reflecting the complexities and moral conflicts of the medieval period.

Language and Style

Middle English literature reveals a transition from Old English's alliterative verse to a more flexible style influenced by French and Latin. Rhymed verse and metrical innovations became prominent, allowing for greater creativity in storytelling and expression. Middle English itself evolved, absorbing words and grammar from Norman French, creating a richer, more versatile language that could accommodate both formal and colloquial expression.

Notable Themes and Symbolism in Middle English Literature

1. **The Quest**: Many Middle English romances involve quests, whether for personal glory, spiritual insight, or adventure. In works like *Sir Gawain and the Green Knight*, the quest structure allows characters to test their virtues and confront their flaws.
2. **Moral Allegory**: Works like *Piers Plowman* use allegorical characters to symbolize moral virtues and vices. Allegory served as a teaching tool, using symbolic storytelling to convey Christian lessons about virtue, sin, and redemption.
3. **Courtly Love**: Inspired by French tradition, courtly love is a recurring theme, exploring idealized, often unattainable love. This concept appears in both secular romances and moral tales, shaping relationships between knights and ladies in ways that highlight virtue, loyalty, and sacrifice.
4. **Religious Mysticism**: Mystical writings, such as those by Julian of Norwich, explored personal, often visionary experiences of God's love and grace. These works reflected a deepening personal faith and were instrumental in shaping devotional literature.

Legacy of Middle English Literature

The Middle English period was essential in shaping the English literary tradition. Chaucer's *The Canterbury Tales* established a foundation for English storytelling and the use of vernacular language, inspiring later writers such as William Shakespeare. The themes and styles developed in Middle English literature, from allegorical storytelling to chivalric ideals, continued to resonate in Renaissance literature and beyond.

The blend of secular and religious literature also laid the groundwork for exploring complex human experiences, from moral choices to questions of faith, loyalty, and justice. Middle English literature's rich diversity and depth made it a foundational era in English letters, bridging the ancient with the emerging modern world and leaving a lasting influence on English storytelling.

Middle English literature captures the dynamic and transformative spirit of a time marked by linguistic, social, and cultural evolution. From Chaucer's lively portrayals of medieval life to Malory's tales of heroism and sacrifice, Middle English literature offers a compelling window into the human condition. It reflects the struggles, beliefs, and values of a society undergoing profound change, making it a cornerstone of English literary heritage and a testament to the enduring power of storytelling.

CHAPTER IV

The Renaissance (1500–1660): Shakespeare and His Contemporaries

The Renaissance was a period of unprecedented cultural growth and intellectual exploration that swept across Europe and transformed English literature. Influenced by the revival of classical learning, humanism, and new philosophical ideas, this era witnessed the emergence of some of the most celebrated authors and works in English literature. William Shakespeare, Christopher Marlowe, Edmund Spenser, and Ben Jonson, among others, brought English poetry, drama, and prose to new heights, crafting works that continue to resonate with readers and audiences today.

Historical and Cultural Context

The English Renaissance began in the early 16th century, inspired by the Italian Renaissance, which had started about a century earlier. This period coincided with major historical events, including the Reformation, which led to religious upheaval, and the reigns of influential monarchs such as Henry VIII, Elizabeth I, and James I. The Renaissance in England encouraged a spirit of inquiry, intellectual freedom, and creative expression that fostered literary experimentation.

Humanism, an intellectual movement that focused on the study of classical texts and emphasized human potential and achievements, played a central role in the English

Renaissance. This shift in thought encouraged writers to explore themes of individual identity, moral integrity, and the complexities of human experience, which shaped the literature of the period.

Major Themes and Characteristics of Renaissance Literature

1. **Humanism and Individualism**: Renaissance literature celebrated the human spirit and explored human potential, often focusing on personal identity, moral conflict, and the pursuit of knowledge. Characters and plots reflected human complexity, and writers delved into themes such as ambition, love, revenge, and justice.
2. **Classical Influence**: Renaissance writers drew inspiration from Greek and Roman classics, reinterpreting mythological, philosophical, and historical subjects for new audiences. This influence is evident in the use of classical references and themes throughout Renaissance poetry, drama, and prose.
3. **Innovation in Poetic Forms**: The Renaissance saw the development of new poetic forms, such as the sonnet, which allowed poets to explore love, nature, and the inner workings of the mind. This era also marked the refinement of blank verse, which became a dominant form in English drama.
4. **Religious and Political Reflections**: Many Renaissance works were shaped by the political and religious turmoil of the time, including the Protestant Reformation and the shifts in monarchy. Writers used literature to comment on social and political issues, often with nuanced or symbolic critiques of power and authority.

5. **Theatrical Expression**: Renaissance drama flourished, with playwrights like Shakespeare and Marlowe experimenting with character development, language, and dramatic structure. Public theaters, such as the Globe, provided a space for diverse audiences to experience these works, which were often infused with wit, emotion, and philosophical reflection.

Key Authors and Works

1. William Shakespeare (1564–1616)

William Shakespeare, perhaps the most renowned writer in the English language, created a body of work that has endured for centuries. His plays cover a wide range of genres, including tragedies, comedies, and histories. Shakespeare's ability to capture universal themes and human emotions makes his works timeless.

- **Tragedies**: Shakespeare's tragedies, including *Hamlet*, *Othello*, *King Lear*, and *Macbeth*, examine themes of ambition, betrayal, love, and power. These plays explore the darker aspects of human nature, portraying characters who are complex and deeply flawed.
- **Comedies**: Shakespeare's comedies, such as *A Midsummer Night's Dream*, *Much Ado About Nothing*, and *Twelfth Night*, often focus on love, mistaken identities, and humorous misunderstandings. Through comedy, Shakespeare examines social norms and human folly.
- **Histories**: Shakespeare's historical plays, such as *Henry IV*, *Henry V*, and *Richard III*, depict the lives of English kings and reflect on themes of leadership, legitimacy,

and power. These plays were both patriotic and critical, capturing the complexities of political ambition.

Shakespeare also wrote sonnets, a collection of 154 poems that explore themes of love, beauty, time, and mortality. His mastery of language, structure, and insight into human nature solidified his status as one of the greatest poets of the Renaissance.

2. Christopher Marlowe (1564–1593)

Christopher Marlowe was one of Shakespeare's most prominent contemporaries and a key figure in English Renaissance drama. Marlowe's works, including *Doctor Faustus*, *Tamburlaine*, and *The Jew of Malta*, are characterized by bold characters, eloquent verse, and philosophical themes.

- *Doctor Faustus*: This play tells the story of a scholar who sells his soul to the devil in exchange for knowledge and power. *Doctor Faustus* explores themes of ambition, hubris, and the consequences of moral compromise, reflecting Renaissance concerns with the limits of human knowledge and the dangers of unchecked desire.

Marlowe's use of blank verse and his tragic vision of human aspiration influenced later playwrights, including Shakespeare.

3. Edmund Spenser (1552–1599)

Edmund Spenser was an influential poet known for his epic poem *The Faerie Queene*, an allegorical work celebrating the virtues of a noble knight and the reign of Queen Elizabeth I. Spenser's work is notable for its complexity, blending elements of chivalric romance, Christian allegory, and moral philosophy.

- *The Faerie Queene*: This unfinished epic poem follows the adventures of several knights, each representing different virtues. *The Faerie Queene* reflects Renaissance ideals of chivalry, virtue, and loyalty, as well as Spenser's deep love for England and Queen Elizabeth.

Spenser developed the Spenserian stanza, a nine-line stanzaic form that became widely influential in English poetry.

4. Ben Jonson (1572–1637)

Ben Jonson, a playwright and poet, was known for his satirical comedies and adherence to classical principles of drama. Jonson's comedies, including *Volpone* and *The Alchemist*, critiqued social manners and moral corruption, often with sharp wit and moral insight.

- *Volpone*: In this play, Jonson satirizes greed and deception through the story of a Venetian nobleman who pretends to be on his deathbed to exploit the greed of those around him. Jonson's keen observations on human folly and his structured, carefully crafted language make him one of the leading figures of Renaissance drama.

Jonson also produced court masques, elaborate performances that combined music, dance, and poetry, showcasing his versatility and collaboration with contemporary artists.

Language and Style

Renaissance literature introduced greater flexibility and expressiveness in English. Poets and playwrights experimented with language, using it to explore human psychology and social dynamics. Blank verse became the preferred medium for drama, allowing for greater fluidity and emotional depth. Sonnets and other lyrical forms grew in popularity, providing a means for exploring personal themes, such as love, nature, and morality.

Symbolism and Themes in Renaissance Literature

1. **The Tragic Hero**: The Renaissance tragic hero, often seen in Shakespeare and Marlowe's works, is a character of noble birth who possesses a tragic flaw (or *hamartia*) that leads to their downfall. The exploration of fate versus free will, as well as the impact of character flaws, is central to these tragedies.
2. **The Supernatural**: Renaissance literature often incorporates the supernatural, whether through ghosts, witches, or magical elements, to explore psychological and ethical themes. For instance, the witches in *Macbeth* foreshadow Macbeth's tragic path, symbolizing the influence of fate and ambition.
3. **Human Conflict**: Renaissance literature delves into the conflicts that arise from ambition, jealousy, love, and revenge. These emotions drive plots and create complex characters who wrestle with moral dilemmas, reflecting the Renaissance fascination with human nature and ethics.
4. **The Power of Rhetoric**: Many Renaissance works display a fascination with language and persuasion. Characters such as Hamlet, Richard III, and Iago use language to manipulate, deceive, or express deep

emotion, highlighting the power of words.

Legacy of Renaissance Literature

The Renaissance established a foundation for modern English literature, defining narrative forms, poetic structures, and dramatic techniques that would shape subsequent literary periods. Shakespeare's characters, Marlowe's tragic vision, and Spenser's allegorical poetry all contributed to a rich literary heritage that explores universal themes of human experience.

The Renaissance also introduced the notion of the individual as central to literature, emphasizing complex characters with nuanced emotions and moral conflicts. This shift created a more introspective and psychologically rich literature, setting the stage for later developments in the novel and modern drama.

Renaissance literature represents a golden age in English letters, a time when writers expanded the boundaries of language and storytelling to explore timeless questions about human nature, morality, and destiny. The works of Shakespeare, Marlowe, Spenser, and their contemporaries continue to captivate readers, offering insights into the human condition and inspiring generations of writers and artists. Through their innovative forms, memorable characters, and profound themes, Renaissance authors left an indelible mark on the history of English literature.

CHAPTER V

The Restoration and 18th Century (1660–1780): Satire and the Rise of the Novel

The Restoration and 18th-century period in English literature was one of lively change and innovation, marked by the return of the monarchy, the rise of the middle class, and a growing interest in human nature, society, and personal relationships. Literature from this era is notable for its sharp wit, satirical edge, and social commentary, reflecting the period's shifting cultural landscape. Two significant developments stand out: the rise of satire as a prominent literary form and the emergence of the English novel, a new genre that would go on to become one of the most influential forms in literature.

Historical and Cultural Context

In 1660, the monarchy was restored in England under Charles II after the Interregnum, a period of Puritan rule under Oliver Cromwell. The Restoration ushered in a new era of permissiveness and opulence, a reaction to the austere morality of the Puritans. This period saw the revival of the theater, which had been banned under Cromwell, and a renewed interest in social and literary freedoms. The 18th century also witnessed political shifts, with the expansion of the British Empire, the rise of the middle class, and an increasing focus on scientific and intellectual inquiry, known as the Enlightenment.

During this period, England's literature began to address contemporary society with a focus on wit, humor, and moral critique. Writers turned their attention to the absurdities and injustices of human behavior, social structures, and political institutions, often using satire to expose hypocrisy and promote rational thought.

Key Characteristics and Themes

1. **Satire and Social Critique**: Satire became a dominant form of expression as writers used humor, irony, and exaggeration to critique social, political, and moral issues. Authors like Jonathan Swift and Alexander Pope employed satire to address the corruption and absurdity they saw in society, including politics, science, and religion.
2. **The Rise of the Novel**: The 18th century saw the development of the novel, a genre that allowed for greater exploration of individual psychology, social relationships, and daily life. Writers like Daniel Defoe, Samuel Richardson, and Henry Fielding experimented with plot, character, and narrative voice, creating realistic stories that reflected the experiences and concerns of the rising middle class.
3. **Rationalism and Enlightenment Thinking**: Influenced by the Enlightenment, writers emphasized reason, logic, and empiricism. Literature often promoted values like progress, tolerance, and individualism, while rejecting superstition and dogma.
4. **Exploration of Morality and Virtue**: Many literary works examined moral and ethical questions, particularly in relation to personal behavior and social

responsibility. Writers explored what it meant to live a virtuous life and critiqued characters or behaviors that fell short of these ideals.

Key Authors and Works

1. John Dryden (1631–1700)

John Dryden was a significant figure in Restoration literature, known for his poetry, plays, and criticism. As the first poet laureate of England, he set the tone for Restoration literature with his polished, formal style and his ability to capture the mood of the age.

- *Absalom and Achitophel*: This satirical poem uses a Biblical story to comment on the political crisis surrounding the Exclusion Bill, which sought to prevent James, Duke of York, from becoming king. Dryden's work exemplifies the use of satire to address political and moral issues indirectly.
- *Mac Flecknoe*: Another famous satire, this poem mocks Dryden's literary rival Thomas Shadwell, showcasing Dryden's wit and mastery of poetic form. It reflects the competitiveness and rivalries among writers during this period.

2. Jonathan Swift (1667–1745)

Jonathan Swift was one of the greatest satirists of the period, known for his biting critiques of society and his darkly humorous approach to human folly and vice. His works often explored themes of human irrationality, corruption, and the dangers of unchecked power.

- *Gulliver's Travels*: Swift's best-known work, this satirical novel follows Lemuel Gulliver's fantastical journeys to imaginary lands. Each journey offers a satire of different aspects of human nature and society, from the petty politics of Lilliput to the rationalism of the Houyhnhnms, offering a critique of European, particularly English, society.
- *A Modest Proposal*: In this scathing pamphlet, Swift uses extreme irony to suggest that the poor should sell their children as food to the rich to solve poverty. Swift's work is a powerful satire on the dehumanization of the poor and the moral failings of the upper classes.

3. Alexander Pope (1688–1744)

Alexander Pope was a poet and satirist known for his sharp wit and moral insight. His works often criticized social norms, artistic pretensions, and the moral failings of his contemporaries.

- *The Rape of the Lock*: This mock-epic poem satirizes the trivial concerns of the aristocracy by presenting a petty quarrel between two families over a lock of hair as an epic struggle. Pope's work combines humor and elegance, highlighting the vanity and superficiality of high society.
- *An Essay on Man*: In this philosophical poem, Pope explores the nature of humanity, attempting to reconcile the presence of suffering with the idea of a benevolent God. The poem reflects Enlightenment values of reason and order, presenting humanity as a small but purposeful part of a larger divine plan.

4. Daniel Defoe (1660–1731)

Daniel Defoe is often considered one of the first novelists in English literature. His works offer realistic portrayals of individual experience, particularly in relation to survival, personal growth, and moral responsibility.

- *Robinson Crusoe:* This novel follows the adventures of a man stranded on a deserted island, exploring themes of self-reliance, resourcefulness, and faith. Defoe's realistic style and focus on the psychological and moral growth of his protagonist set the stage for the development of the novel.
- *Moll Flanders:* This picaresque novel tells the story of a woman who navigates life through a series of adventures and moral challenges. Defoe's work offers a complex portrayal of gender, morality, and social class, highlighting the challenges faced by women in a patriarchal society.

5. Samuel Richardson (1689–1761) and Henry Fielding (1707–1754)

Richardson and Fielding were instrumental in shaping the novel as a genre, offering distinct approaches to storytelling.

- *Pamela* by Samuel Richardson: This epistolary novel tells the story of a young maidservant who resists her master's advances and ultimately marries him. Richardson's work explores themes of virtue, class, and power, presenting a moralistic view of female virtue.
- *Tom Jones* by Henry Fielding: Fielding's novel is a comic, picaresque story that follows the adventures of a foundling named Tom Jones. Fielding's realistic characters, social critique, and use of humor highlight

the moral complexities of 18th-century life and mark a significant contribution to the development of the English novel.

Language and Style

The Restoration and 18th-century literature is characterized by clarity, wit, and balance. Writers favored a straightforward style, often modeled after classical Greek and Roman works, with an emphasis on clarity, elegance, and precision. The rise of the essay as a literary form, pioneered by writers like Joseph Addison and Richard Steele, also reflects the period's commitment to rational discussion and moral instruction.

Notable Themes and Symbolism in 18th-Century Literature

1. **Vanity and Hypocrisy**: Satirical works often targeted the vanity, hypocrisy, and superficiality of individuals and institutions. Through humor and irony, writers like Swift and Pope critiqued the pretensions of the aristocracy, the clergy, and the emerging middle class.
2. **Virtue and Morality**: Many works from this period explored questions of virtue, often presenting idealized characters who embody moral qualities or flawed characters who serve as cautionary tales. Richardson's *Pamela* and Defoe's *Robinson Crusoe* both reflect a strong moral dimension.
3. **Social Class and Power**: The growing influence of the middle class is reflected in literature's interest in social

mobility, wealth, and status. Novels such as *Tom Jones* and *Moll Flanders* explore the lives of characters who navigate the complexities of social hierarchy.

4. **The Pursuit of Knowledge and Reason**: Enlightenment ideals emphasized the importance of reason, science, and intellectual inquiry. Literature from this period often reflects a fascination with human knowledge, personal improvement, and the idea of human progress.

Legacy of Restoration and 18th-Century Literature

This period in English literature laid the foundation for modern satire, journalism, and the novel. The sharp social critique and satirical humor developed by Swift, Pope, and others influenced subsequent writers, including Charles Dickens and Mark Twain. The novel, meanwhile, evolved into a central genre for exploring individual experience, social relationships, and the complexities of modern life.

The Restoration and 18th century were defining moments in English literature, producing works that reflected and shaped the society of the time. Through satire, wit, and the newly emerging form of the novel, writers offered nuanced portrayals of human nature, morality, and social structures. The literature of this era, from the scathing satires of Swift and Pope to the realistic novels of Defoe and Fielding, remains influential, capturing the tensions and transformations of a rapidly changing world.

CHAPTER VI

The Romantic Period (1780–1832): Wordsworth, Keats, and the Spirit of Rebellion

The Romantic Period in English literature was a time of intense creativity and change, marked by a profound shift in the way writers approached themes of nature, imagination, emotion, and the self. Sparked by political revolutions, rapid industrialization, and societal transformation, Romantic writers reacted against the Enlightenment emphasis on reason, instead celebrating the power of individual expression, the beauty of nature, and the mystery of the supernatural. William Wordsworth, John Keats, and other key figures became passionate voices of this movement, emphasizing the importance of personal experience, poetic freedom, and a rebellion against societal conventions.

Historical and Cultural Context

The Romantic Period began in the late 18th century, a time of social and political upheaval that included the American Revolution (1775–1783) and the French Revolution (1789–1799). The effects of these revolutions, coupled with the rapid growth of industry, left a deep impact on the public consciousness and inspired writers to question authority, embrace individual freedom, and explore revolutionary ideas.

As a reaction against the rationality and order of the Enlightenment, Romanticism emphasized emotion, intuition, and the sublime beauty of nature. Writers sought to transcend societal restrictions, creating works that championed the human spirit, celebrated natural beauty, and examined the depths of human imagination. The Romantic Period is also known for its exploration of the supernatural, the mystical, and the Gothic, as well as its fascination with medieval themes and folk traditions.

Key Themes and Characteristics of Romantic Literature

1. **Nature as a Source of Inspiration**: Romantic writers revered nature as a spiritual and healing force. Unlike the Enlightenment view of nature as a mechanism to be understood, Romantics saw it as alive, mystical, and a source of personal renewal. They depicted nature as a means of self-discovery and a reflection of human emotion.

2. **The Power of Imagination**: The Romantics valued imagination over reason, viewing it as a pathway to deeper understanding and transcendence. Imagination was seen as a creative force that could connect the individual to the divine or the infinite, often exploring themes that lay beyond the reach of logical thought.

3. **Emotion and Individual Experience**: Romantic literature placed a high value on emotional intensity and personal expression. Writers explored the depths of the human soul, delving into love, melancholy, joy, and despair. Poetry and prose often depicted intense, sometimes even tumultuous feelings.

4. **The Supernatural and the Gothic**: Fascination with the supernatural, the mysterious, and the grotesque is evident in much Romantic literature. Many writers incorporated Gothic elements, including haunted settings, supernatural beings, and themes of terror, to delve into psychological and spiritual conflict.

5. **Rebellion Against Convention**: The Romantic spirit was one of defiance and nonconformity. Many Romantic writers rejected traditional societal structures and norms, promoting ideals of personal freedom, creativity, and authenticity. This spirit of rebellion is seen in their critiques of industrialization, social hierarchy, and organized religion.

6. **The Noble Outcast and Byronic Hero**: Romantic literature often features characters who are outsiders or rebels, struggling against social norms and personal flaws. The "Byronic hero," named after Lord Byron's characters, is a complex, charismatic figure marked by a sense of rebellion, mystery, and inner torment.

Key Authors and Works

1. William Wordsworth (1770–1850)

William Wordsworth was a central figure in the Romantic movement and is often celebrated for his deep reverence for nature and his pioneering use of simple, everyday language in poetry. His partnership with Samuel Taylor Coleridge and their publication of *Lyrical Ballads* (1798) is often seen as the formal beginning of the Romantic movement in English literature.

- *Lyrical Ballads*(1798): This collection, co-authored with Coleridge, is considered a manifesto of Romantic ideals. Wordsworth's poems, such as "Lines Composed a Few Miles Above Tintern Abbey" and "We Are Seven," emphasized themes of nature, simplicity, and the innocence of childhood.
- *"I Wandered Lonely as a Cloud"*: Also known as "Daffodils," this poem captures Wordsworth's admiration for the beauty of nature and the deep connection he felt with his surroundings. The poem expresses the uplifting power of nature and its lasting impact on memory and spirit.
- *The Prelude*: An autobiographical epic, *The Prelude* recounts Wordsworth's spiritual development and his profound relationship with nature. The poem explores themes of memory, growth, and the influence of nature on the mind.

2. Samuel Taylor Coleridge (1772–1834)

Samuel Taylor Coleridge was a poet, philosopher, and critic known for his imaginative vision and fascination with the supernatural. Coleridge's works often explore themes of mystery, spirituality, and psychological conflict.

- *"The Rime of the Ancient Mariner"*: This narrative poem tells the story of a mariner cursed after killing an albatross. The poem is rich with supernatural imagery and explores themes of guilt, redemption, and the sacredness of nature.
- *"Kubla Khan"*: Written after a vivid dream, this unfinished poem transports readers to an exotic and mystical realm. *"Kubla Khan"* is a celebration of imagination and the beauty of creation, emphasizing

Coleridge's fascination with the unconscious mind.

3. John Keats (1795–1821)

John Keats, known for his sensuous imagery and exploration of beauty, was a leading voice in the later years of the Romantic movement. Though his career was tragically short, Keats left behind a legacy of poems that embody Romantic ideals of beauty, mortality, and passion.

- *"Ode to a Nightingale"*: This ode is one of Keats's most celebrated works, exploring the tension between the eternal beauty of art and the transient nature of human life. The nightingale becomes a symbol of immortality and transcendence, contrasting with the speaker's awareness of mortality.
- *"Ode on a Grecian Urn"*: Another well-known ode, this poem meditates on the nature of beauty, art, and eternity. The urn represents a timeless ideal, prompting the famous line, "Beauty is truth, truth beauty."
- *"To Autumn"*: Keats's ode to autumn celebrates the beauty of the season while also reflecting themes of maturity, harvest, and the inevitability of death. The poem's imagery is richly evocative, capturing the fullness and ripeness of life.

4. Lord Byron (1788–1824)

George Gordon, Lord Byron, was known for his flamboyant personality, passionate love affairs, and rebellious nature, both in life and in his poetry. His creation of the "Byronic hero" left a lasting impact on literature.

- *Childe Harold's Pilgrimage*: This semi-autobiographical poem features a protagonist who is disillusioned with society and embarks on a journey through Europe. The character embodies the Romantic ideal of the noble outcast, torn between cynicism and longing for meaning.

- ***Don Juan***: Byron's mock-epic poem presents the legendary lover Don Juan in a new light, as a charming and naive young man. The poem combines humor, satire, and social critique, challenging traditional moral and social norms.

5. Percy Bysshe Shelley (1792–1822)

Percy Bysshe Shelley was a radical thinker, political activist, and poet who challenged conventions with his idealism and advocacy for social justice. His poetry often focuses on themes of change, rebellion, and the transformative power of love and imagination.

- ***"Ode to the West Wind"***: In this powerful poem, Shelley calls on the west wind as a symbol of change and transformation. The speaker desires to be an agent of change, expressing a desire for personal and social renewal.
- ***Prometheus Unbound***: This lyrical drama reimagines the myth of Prometheus, who defied the gods to give fire to humanity. The work celebrates the human spirit's resilience and resistance to tyranny.

Language and Style in Romantic Poetry

Romantic writers favored a language that was direct, evocative, and emotionally charged. They sought to connect with readers on an emotional level, often rejecting the formal structures and decorum of previous literary styles. Imagery in Romantic literature is frequently lush and sensory, bringing natural landscapes and experiences vividly to life. Wordsworth's conversational language, Coleridge's dreamlike visions, and Keats's rich sensory details illustrate the diverse stylistic approaches within the Romantic movement.

Key Themes and Symbols in Romantic Literature

1. **Nature and the Sublime**: Nature is a central theme in Romantic literature, often depicted as a source of awe, mystery, and inspiration. The concept of the sublime, which involves feelings of awe and terror inspired by nature's grandeur, is frequently explored.
2. **The Quest for Transcendence**: Many Romantic works reflect a yearning for transcendence and a connection to something greater than the self, whether through nature, art, or imagination.
3. **Mortality and Melancholy**: Romantic poets often pondered the fleeting nature of life and the inevitability of death, themes particularly prominent in the works of Keats and Shelley.
4. **The Supernatural and Mystical**: Elements of the supernatural and mystical frequently appear, revealing a fascination with the unknown and the mysterious forces that shape human experience.

Legacy of the Romantic Period

The Romantic movement forever altered the landscape of English literature, laying the groundwork for modern poetry and prose. Its emphasis on individual expression, imagination, and the emotional richness of human experience continues to influence writers and artists today. Romantics challenged societal

CHAPTER VII

The Victorian Era (1832–1901): Social Change and the Novel

The Victorian era, named after Queen Victoria's reign, was a period of dramatic social, cultural, and political change. Spanning from 1832 to 1901, this period in English literature saw the rise of the novel as the dominant literary form. Writers grappled with the challenges of industrialization, urbanization, colonialism, and the evolving role of science and religion. This era produced some of the most famous English novels, as authors responded to the rapid changes in society and questioned long-held conventions.

Historical and Cultural Context

The Victorian period was marked by significant transformations. Britain emerged as the world's leading industrial power, and cities swelled with an influx of people seeking work. The Industrial Revolution brought wealth to many, but also introduced significant challenges, including the rise of poverty, child labor, and harsh working conditions. The era also witnessed the expansion of the British Empire, leading to debates about colonialism, race, and empire.

At the same time, Victorian society was marked by strict moral codes, social class distinctions, and an obsession with respectability. Religious faith was tested by the scientific advancements of the time, particularly Charles

Darwin's theory of evolution, which sparked debates over the relationship between science and religion. Writers in this period engaged with these tensions, often using the novel as a medium to reflect upon and critique the complexities of Victorian life.

The Rise of the Novel

The Victorian era saw the rise of the novel as the most popular and influential literary genre. While novels had existed before, they became increasingly accessible and widely read during this period. The rise of the middle class, the spread of literacy, and the development of the publishing industry all contributed to the popularity of the novel. Serialization in periodicals also became common, allowing readers to enjoy novels in installments before the full works were published.

Writers such as Charles Dickens, George Eliot, Thomas Hardy, and the Brontë sisters are just a few of the most influential figures of this time, and their works remain essential to the canon of English literature.

Key Themes in Victorian Literature

1. **Social Class and the Struggles of the Poor**: One of the central themes in Victorian literature is the impact of social class on individuals. The Industrial Revolution created a stark divide between the wealthy and the working class, and many writers addressed issues of poverty, exploitation, and social justice. Dickens, in particular, often depicted the hardships faced by the poor in his novels.

2. **Morality and Respectability**: The Victorian era was characterized by a strict moral code, especially regarding issues like marriage, sexuality, and propriety. Writers frequently explored the tensions between individual desires and societal expectations, as well as the consequences of breaking these moral codes.

3. **The Role of Women**: The role of women was another key topic in Victorian literature. While women were expected to embody the ideals of domesticity and virtue, the emerging feminist movement began to challenge these roles. Writers like the Brontë sisters and George Eliot examined the limitations placed on women and the struggles for independence and self-expression.

4. **Industrialization and Its Effects**: The rapid industrialization of Britain during the Victorian period had a profound impact on both the economy and society. While industrialization led to economic growth, it also created widespread social problems, including poor working conditions, overcrowding in cities, and environmental degradation. These issues are explored in the works of authors such as Elizabeth Gaskell and Charles Dickens.

5. **Science and Religion**: The Victorian era was also a time of significant scientific advancement, most notably with the publication of Charles Darwin's *On the Origin of Species* (1859). The theory of evolution raised questions about the nature of humanity, creation, and the existence of God. Literature during this time reflects the tension between religious faith and scientific discovery, with writers examining how these forces shaped people's views on life and society.

6. **The Gothic and the Supernatural**: While the Victorian period is often associated with realism, there was also

a continued interest in the Gothic and the supernatural. The late-Victorian era saw a resurgence of Gothic elements in literature, with themes of mystery, madness, and the macabre appearing in works such as Robert Louis Stevenson's *Dr. Jekyll and Mr. Hyde* and Bram Stoker's *Dracula*.

7. **Colonialism and Empire**: As the British Empire expanded during the Victorian period, many writers grappled with issues of empire, race, and the treatment of colonized peoples. The literature of this time often reflects the anxieties surrounding imperialism, with some writers critiquing the brutality of colonial rule, while others celebrated Britain's global dominance.

Key Authors and Works

1. Charles Dickens (1812–1870)

Charles Dickens is perhaps the most famous Victorian author, known for his vivid depictions of Victorian society and his social criticism. His works often center on the plight of the poor and the injustices of the social system.

- *Oliver Twist* (1837–1839): One of Dickens's most famous works, this novel tells the story of a young orphan who faces the harsh realities of life in a workhouse and the criminal underworld of London. *Oliver Twist* critiques the treatment of the poor and the injustices of the Victorian class system.
- *A Tale of Two Cities* (1859): Set during the French Revolution, this novel explores themes of resurrection, sacrifice, and social injustice. The famous opening line, "It was the best of times, it was the worst of times,"

reflects the stark contrasts between the aristocracy and the lower classes during a period of revolution.

- *Great Expectations* (1860–1861): This novel follows the life of Pip, an orphan who grows up with lofty ambitions but is disillusioned by his pursuit of wealth and social status. *Great Expectations* explores themes of guilt, redemption, and social class.

2. George Eliot (Mary Ann Evans, 1819–1880)

George Eliot, the pen name of Mary Ann Evans, was one of the most important novelists of the Victorian era. Her works often focused on moral dilemmas, social change, and the psychology of her characters.

- *Middlemarch* (1871–1872): A complex novel set in a fictional English town, *Middlemarch* explores themes of marriage, politics, and social change. Eliot examines the limitations of the Victorian social structure and the consequences of individual choices.
- *Silas Marner* (1861): This novel tells the story of a miserly weaver who, after being betrayed by his community, finds redemption through his love for a child. It explores themes of community, isolation, and transformation.

3. The Brontë Sisters

The Brontë sisters—Charlotte, Emily, and Anne—produced some of the most enduring works of Victorian literature. Their novels often focus on themes of passion, social class, and the restrictions placed on women.

- *Jane Eyre* (1847) by Charlotte Brontë: This novel tells the story of an orphaned girl who becomes a governess and falls in love with her employer, Mr. Rochester. *Jane Eyre* explores themes of love, morality, and the struggles of women to find independence in a restrictive society.

- ***Wuthering Heights* (1847)** by Emily Brontë: A dark and passionate tale of love, obsession, and revenge, *Wuthering Heights* is set on the Yorkshire moors and explores the destructive power of unrequited love.
- ***The Tenant of Wildfell Hall* (1848)** by Anne Brontë: This novel deals with issues of alcoholism, domestic abuse, and the plight of women trapped in abusive marriages. It is a pioneering work in feminist literature.

4. Thomas Hardy (1840–1928)

Thomas Hardy was a novelist and poet known for his exploration of the darker aspects of rural life and the inevitability of fate. His works often depict the struggles of individuals against an indifferent or hostile society.

- ***Tess of the d'Urbervilles* (1891)**: This novel tells the tragic story of Tess, a woman who faces the consequences of her sexual victimization in a harsh and unforgiving society. It critiques the social mores surrounding women and class in Victorian England.
- ***Jude the Obscure* (1895)**: Hardy's final novel, *Jude the Obscure*, addresses issues of class, education, and marriage. The protagonist, Jude, struggles against the rigid class system, yet his attempts to better himself lead to personal tragedy.

5. Robert Louis Stevenson (1850–1894)

Stevenson's works are known for their exploration of morality, duality, and the human psyche. His works often blend adventure with psychological insight.

- ***The Strange Case of Dr. Jekyll and Mr. Hyde* (1886)**: This novella explores the duality of human nature, as Dr. Jekyll, a respected doctor, transforms into the villainous Mr. Hyde. The story grapples with the conflict between good and evil within a single individual.
- ***Treasure Island* (1883)**: One of the most famous adventure novels, *Treasure Island* tells the story of a young boy's search for treasure on a remote island, with memorable characters like Long John Silver.

Victorian Novels and Social Commentary

Victorian novels often serve as a mirror to society, reflecting the era's most pressing issues. They provide a window into the complexities of class, gender, morality, and the consequences of rapid industrialization. The novel form allowed writers to develop intricate plots, complex characters, and multi-layered social commentary. As such, Victorian novels remain essential in understanding the social dynamics and cultural conflicts of the 19th century.

Legacy of the Victorian Era

The Victorian era established many of the literary conventions that continue to shape the novel today. Its focus on character development, moral complexity, and social critique left an indelible mark on the literary world. The works of Victorian authors continue to be studied and appreciated for their depth, insight, and historical relevance, offering rich explorations of the human condition.

CHAPTER VIII

The Modernist Period (1901–1945): Breaking Boundaries in Form and Style

The Modernist period in literature, which spans from 1901 to 1945, is marked by an intense period of experimentation and innovation. In response to the rapid changes of the 20th century—including the upheavals of war, the rise of industrialization, technological advances, and shifts in social structures—writers sought to break away from the established conventions of the past. This era witnessed a dramatic shift in the way literature was written and read, as Modernist writers sought to reflect the fragmented, disorienting experience of modern life.

Historical and Cultural Context

The early 20th century was a time of profound change. The two World Wars (1914–1918 and 1939–1945) reshaped global politics and economies, while technological advancements such as the automobile, the airplane, and the telephone revolutionized communication and transportation. The horrors of war, the rise of fascism, and the social turmoil of the interwar years left many disillusioned with the old ways of thinking and living.

Socially and culturally, the Modernist period coincided with the rise of new ideologies. Feminism gained momentum, and there was an increasing challenge to traditional roles of women in society. The rise of psychoanalysis, particularly the theories of Sigmund Freud, and the developments in quantum physics, such as Albert Einstein's theory of relativity, also contributed to a sense of uncertainty and relativism in knowledge. These shifts in science, philosophy, and society all found expression in literature.

At the same time, Modernism also represented a reaction against the constraints of Victorian morality and traditionalism. Writers sought to explore new forms of artistic expression, creating works that were fragmented, non-linear, and more concerned with inner psychological states than with external actions.

Key Characteristics of Modernist Literature

1. **Stream of Consciousness**: One of the most notable techniques introduced by Modernist writers was the "stream of consciousness," a narrative mode that attempts to capture the continuous flow of thoughts, memories, and sensations in a character's mind. This technique, championed by writers like James Joyce and Virginia Woolf, breaks away from traditional linear storytelling, offering a more fragmented and subjective view of reality.
2. **Nonlinear Narratives**: Modernist writers rejected the traditional structure of beginning, middle, and end. Their works often feature fragmented timelines, shifting perspectives, and a lack of clear resolutions. These techniques reflect the chaos and uncertainty of the modern world.
3. **Alienation and Disillusionment**: The sense of disillusionment that followed the devastation of the

World Wars is central to Modernist literature. Many works reflect feelings of alienation from society, disconnection from past values, and a pervasive sense of despair about the future.

4. **Ambiguity and Multiple Perspectives**: Modernist works often leave questions unanswered or present multiple interpretations, forcing readers to engage with the text in a more active way. This ambiguity reflects the uncertainty of the modern world and challenges readers to question traditional norms and values.

5. **Experiments with Form and Style**: Modernists were not bound by conventional narrative forms. They experimented with language, structure, and genre. This includes the use of fragmented or incomplete narratives, poetry written in free verse, and plays that focus on the internal rather than external actions.

6. **A Focus on the Interior Life**: Unlike the more traditional forms of literature, which often focus on external actions and events, Modernist literature is more concerned with the inner lives of characters. Writers sought to explore the unconscious mind, psychological depth, and the complexities of human consciousness.

7. **Rejection of Realism**: Modernist literature often departs from the detailed realism of 19th-century writers. Instead of focusing on objective external realities, Modernist authors explore the subjective experiences of characters. The external world becomes less important than the internal world of thought, feeling, and perception.

Key Authors and Works

1. James Joyce (1882–1941)

James Joyce is often regarded as one of the most important figures in Modernist literature. His works employ stream of consciousness, symbolic imagery, and experimental narratives to depict the inner workings of the mind.

- *Ulysses* **(1922)**: Perhaps Joyce's most famous work, *Ulysses* follows the experiences of Leopold Bloom over the course of a single day in Dublin. The novel uses stream-of-consciousness techniques, puns, and allusions to classical texts to explore the nature of identity, memory, and the mundane aspects of everyday life. The novel revolutionized the use of language in literature and is considered one of the greatest novels of the 20th century.
- *A Portrait of the Artist as a Young Man* **(1916)**: This semi-autobiographical novel explores the development of Stephen Dedalus, Joyce's alter ego, as he grapples with his identity, family, and religion. It reflects the Modernist exploration of the individual's psychological and emotional growth.

2. Virginia Woolf (1882–1941)

Virginia Woolf is another key Modernist writer whose works delve deeply into the inner thoughts and emotions of her characters. Woolf was instrumental in developing the stream-of-consciousness technique and exploring the subjective experience of consciousness.

- *Mrs. Dalloway* **(1925)**: Set in post-World War I London, *Mrs. Dalloway* follows Clarissa Dalloway as she prepares for a party while reflecting on her past. Woolf employs stream-of-consciousness to provide insight into the characters' inner lives and to explore themes of mental illness, time, and the effects of war.

- ***To the Lighthouse* (1927)**: This novel, considered one of Woolf's masterpieces, examines the lives of the Ramsay family and their guests on a summer vacation. The novel explores themes of time, memory, and the roles of women in society, using shifting perspectives and interior monologue to explore the characters' consciousness.

3. T.S. Eliot (1888–1965)

T.S. Eliot was a poet and playwright whose works reflect the disillusionment of the Modernist era and the search for meaning in a fragmented world. His poetry often addresses themes of alienation, spiritual desolation, and the collapse of traditional values.

- ***The Waste Land* (1922)**: One of the most famous Modernist poems, *The Waste Land* is a fragmented, allusive work that explores the collapse of Western culture in the wake of World War I. The poem uses a wide range of references to mythology, religion, and literature to depict a world devoid of meaning and direction.
- ***The Love Song of J. Alfred Prufrock* (1915)**: This early poem by Eliot introduces the character of J. Alfred Prufrock, a modern man plagued by self-doubt, indecision, and fear of social judgment. The poem explores the inner turmoil and alienation of the individual in the modern world.

4. Franz Kafka (1883–1924)

Though Kafka wrote in German, his works have had a profound influence on Modernist literature in English. His works explore themes of alienation, bureaucracy, and the absurdity of life.

- *The Metamorphosis* **(1915)**: This novella tells the story of Gregor Samsa, who wakes up one morning to find himself transformed into a giant insect. The work explores themes of identity, family, and the individual's struggle to find meaning in a seemingly indifferent world.
- *The Trial* **(1914–1915)**: This novel, left unfinished at Kafka's death, follows Josef K., a man who is arrested and put on trial for an unspecified crime. Kafka's portrayal of a faceless, oppressive legal system reflects the existential anxiety of the Modernist era.

5. William Faulkner (1897–1962)

William Faulkner, an American Modernist writer, is known for his innovative narrative techniques, including stream of consciousness and fragmented timelines. His works often explore the complexities of the American South and the effects of history on individual lives.

- *The Sound and the Fury* **(1929)**: This novel is perhaps Faulkner's most famous work, employing a fragmented narrative structure to depict the decline of the Compson family in the American South. The novel's use of stream-of-consciousness and its non-linear timeline reflect the disorienting nature of time and memory.
- *As I Lay Dying* **(1930)**: This novel tells the story of the Bundren family's journey to bury their deceased mother. Told from multiple viewpoints, the novel

explores themes of death, family, and the personal struggles of each character.

Modernist Literature and Its Legacy

The Modernist period broke away from traditional literary forms, giving writers the freedom to explore new styles, structures, and themes. The innovations of this era have had a lasting impact on literature, influencing writers and poets well beyond the 1945 cutoff of the period. Modernism's exploration of the inner workings of the mind, its experiments with form, and its disillusioned view of modern society all contributed to a body of work that continues to challenge readers and inspire new generations of writers. The period's focus on alienation, subjectivity, and fragmentation has made it central to understanding the complexities of the modern world.

CHAPTER IX

Postmodernism and Contemporary Literature (1945–Present)

The period following World War II marked a shift in literary trends and cultural movements. As a response to the uncertainties and the rapid changes of the 20th century, postmodernism emerged as a dominant literary paradigm, reflecting a complex, fragmented world. Unlike modernism, which sought to find meaning and coherence in a fractured world, postmodernism emphasized the absence of universal truths, celebrating ambiguity, paradox, and the deconstruction of traditional narrative structures.

Postmodernism and contemporary literature (1945–present) have seen the rise of new literary forms, global perspectives, and technological influences that continue to shape the way stories are told and understood.

Historical and Cultural Context

The aftermath of World War II set the stage for a period of intense experimentation and innovation in literature. The war had left much of Europe in ruins, and with the rise of nuclear weapons, the threat of global annihilation loomed large. Social and cultural upheavals, such as the Civil Rights Movement, feminism, postcolonial struggles, and the rise of technology, all played a role in shaping the postwar literary landscape.

- **Cold War Tensions and the Threat of Nuclear War**: The geopolitical divide between the United States and the Soviet Union created a climate of fear and uncertainty. This period saw the emergence of existential anxieties, often expressed in literature through themes of alienation, identity, and the search for meaning in an unpredictable world.
- **Postcolonialism**: The dismantling of European empires and the independence of former colonies gave rise to postcolonial literature, which challenged Eurocentric narratives and explored the effects of colonization on both colonizers and the colonized. Writers such as Chinua Achebe, Salman Rushdie, and Ngũgĩ wa Thiong'o emerged as voices of this global movement.
- **Technological Change**: The rise of television, computers, and the internet changed the way people consumed media. Literature began to reflect the complexities of technology and media in society, as authors experimented with new forms of communication and storytelling.
- **Cultural Movements**: Civil rights, feminist movements, LGBTQ+ rights, and environmentalism all influenced literature during this period. Writers began exploring a wider range of identities, experiences, and social issues, moving beyond the traditional Eurocentric, heteronormative, and male-dominated narratives that had shaped literature for centuries.

Key Characteristics of Postmodern Literature

1. **Intertextuality**: One of the defining features of postmodernism is intertextuality, or the practice of referencing or incorporating other works of literature, art, or pop culture. In postmodern literature, texts often play with and subvert established genres and conventions, acknowledging that no work exists in isolation.

2. **Metafiction**: Postmodern writers often engage in metafiction, or writing that self-consciously comments on its own creation. This may involve breaking the fourth wall, discussing the writing process, or explicitly questioning the relationship between fiction and reality.

3. **Fragmentation**: Postmodern literature often employs fragmented narratives, non-linear structures, and multiple perspectives. Unlike modernism, which used fragmentation to explore the individual's consciousness, postmodernism's fragmentation reflects the breakdown of traditional narrative forms and the rejection of the idea that meaning can be found in any singular, unified structure.

4. **Pastiche**: Postmodern writers often blend or "paste" together elements of different genres, styles, and cultural forms. This is done playfully, often for ironic or humorous effect, challenging the notion of any one "authentic" voice or form.

5. **Playfulness and Irony**: Postmodern literature is often characterized by its sense of playfulness, absurdity, and irony. Writers may use humor and wit to subvert expectations, challenge authority, or critique societal norms.

6. **Self-Reflexivity**: Postmodern works often draw attention to the fact that they are constructions, reminding readers that literature is a human-made

artifact. Authors may question or destabilize the authority of the narrator, highlight the limitations of language, or expose the artifice of literary forms.

7. **Hyperreality**: Postmodern literature, particularly in the works of authors like Jean Baudrillard and Umberto Eco, explores the idea of hyperreality—a state in which the line between reality and representation becomes blurred. In this environment, simulations, media representations, and artificial constructs may be experienced as more "real" than actual reality.

8. **Relativism and Subjectivity**: Postmodernism rejects the idea of absolute truths or universal narratives. Rather than portraying a single objective reality, postmodern texts highlight the multiplicity of viewpoints and the subjective nature of experience.

9. **Absurdism**: Like existentialism, postmodernism often explores the absurdity of life, but with a more pronounced sense of humor. The postmodern condition is one of fragmentation, uncertainty, and meaninglessness, but authors often approach these themes with irony, absurdity, or playful detachment.

Key Authors and Works

1. Thomas Pynchon (1937–Present)

Thomas Pynchon is considered one of the leading figures in postmodern literature, known for his complex, fragmented narratives and his blend of historical fiction with science fiction, popular culture, and philosophical speculation.

- *Gravity's Rainbow* (1973): This novel is a sprawling, multi-layered work set during the final months of World War II. It incorporates elements of historical fiction, conspiracy theories, and speculative fiction, and is known for its dense, fragmented narrative and its exploration of the relationship between technology, power, and human agency.
- *The Crying of Lot 49* (1966): This shorter novel is a work of paranoid fiction, following Oedipa Maas as she uncovers a cryptic conspiracy involving an ancient postal system. The novel explores themes of communication, media, and the difficulty of discerning truth in a world of constant information overload.

2. Don DeLillo *(1936–Present)*

Don DeLillo is a key figure in contemporary American literature, known for his exploration of the effects of technology, mass media, and consumerism on modern life.

- *White Noise* (1985): This novel follows the lives of the Babette family as they navigate a world dominated by media saturation, consumer culture, and environmental threats. The novel blends dark humor with a critique of contemporary society, exploring the existential anxieties of living in a postmodern, media-driven world.
- *Libra* (1988): A historical novel that blends fiction with real-life events, *Libra* explores the assassination of President John F. Kennedy. The novel interrogates the nature of truth, history, and the narrative construction of events.

3. Kurt Vonnegut (1922–2007)

Kurt Vonnegut's works often blend science fiction, satire, and absurdism, reflecting the postmodern sensibility of questioning authority, truth, and meaning.

- *Slaughterhouse-Five* **(1969)**: One of Vonnegut's best-known works, *Slaughterhouse-Five* is a novel about the bombing of Dresden during World War II. It employs a non-linear narrative structure, incorporating time travel and elements of science fiction, and addresses themes of free will, the horrors of war, and the absurdity of human existence.
- *Cat's Cradle* **(1963)**: This novel satirizes science, religion, and human folly, particularly through the invention of a substance called Ice-Nine, which could potentially destroy the world. Vonnegut's sharp wit and use of absurdity highlight the absurdity and fragility of modern life.

4. Margaret Atwood (1939–Present)
Margaret Atwood is a celebrated Canadian writer whose works explore themes of feminism, dystopia, and the intersection of nature and technology.

- *The Handmaid's Tale* **(1985)**: Set in a dystopian future where women are subjugated by a theocratic government, *The Handmaid's Tale* explores themes of power, gender, and the manipulation of truth. It is considered a major work in postmodern feminist literature.
- *Oryx and Crake* **(2003)**: This novel is part of Atwood's *MaddAddam* trilogy and combines elements of speculative fiction, satire, and environmental concerns. It imagines a future in which genetic engineering and

corporate greed have led to the collapse of humanity.

5. Jeanette Winterson (1959–Present)

Jeanette Winterson is a British author whose works frequently explore themes of gender, sexuality, and identity.

- ***Oranges Are Not the Only Fruit* (1985)**: This semi-autobiographical novel deals with themes of sexual identity, religion, and the coming-of-age of a young lesbian in a strict religious community. The novel's experimental style and structure make it a hallmark of postmodern feminist literature.
- ***Written on the Body* (1992)**: In this novel, Winterson explores the themes of love, loss, and identity through a narrator whose gender remains unspecified. The novel plays with language, narrative conventions, and the idea of love as both a physical and intellectual experience.

Contemporary Literature and Its Impact

Postmodernism and contemporary literature reflect the complexity, uncertainty, and fluidity of the modern world. Writers in this period question traditional narrative forms, challenge ideas of identity and truth, and reflect on the fragmented, often absurd nature of contemporary life. Through experimentation with genre, structure, and perspective, postmodern authors have reshaped the landscape of literary production, paving the way for future innovations in narrative and style. The postmodern ethos of questioning authority and embracing multiplicity has had a profound influence on contemporary literature, allowing it to remain dynamic, diverse, and continuously evolving.

CHAPTER X

Themes and Motifs Across English Literature

English literature is rich with recurring themes and motifs that have persisted across centuries, evolving with each historical and cultural period. These themes often reflect universal human experiences, offering insight into the values, struggles, and ideals of societies throughout time. From the epic sagas of Old English literature to the complexities of modern and contemporary works, these recurring elements shape the literary landscape, helping readers to understand not just the characters and plots, but the deeper concerns and philosophies that drive the narrative.

This chapter explores key themes and motifs that span across English literature, demonstrating their evolution and relevance across different periods.

1. The Struggle Between Good and Evil

One of the most pervasive themes in English literature is the battle between good and evil. This theme often symbolizes moral conflicts, with characters or groups representing either virtue or vice. The struggle is not always clear-cut; instead, it can be ambiguous, offering a nuanced exploration of human nature.

- **Early Examples**: In works like *Beowulf*, the hero's battle against Grendel, Grendel's mother, and the dragon reflects the fight against monstrous evil, where good (Beowulf) triumphs through bravery and strength. The theme of good vs. evil is starkly defined in these early works, but even here, moral complexity can be found in the characters' motivations and actions.

- **In Shakespeare**: This theme is present in plays such as *Macbeth*, where Macbeth's internal struggle between ambition (evil) and guilt (good) reveals the complexities of human morality. Similarly, in *Hamlet*, the conflict between Hamlet's desire for justice (good) and his actions of revenge (which cause collateral damage) complicates the moral landscape.
- **Modern Approaches**: In postmodern literature, this theme becomes less about clear-cut opposites and more about the ambiguity of good and evil. Writers such as *Joseph Conrad* in *Heart of Darkness* present evil not as an external force, but as an inherent part of humanity, questioning the nature of moral absolutism.

2. The Power of Love

Love, in all its forms—romantic, familial, platonic, and self-love—has been a central theme in English literature. From the earliest narratives to the modern age, love has been depicted as a force that shapes characters' destinies, challenges societal norms, and drives both plot and character development.

- **Romantic Love**: In the *Medieval* period, courtly love was explored in works like Geoffrey Chaucer's *The Canterbury Tales* and the *Arthurian Legends*. These stories often portrayed love as an idealized, sometimes unattainable force that demanded sacrifice, loyalty, and devotion. In *Romeo and Juliet* by Shakespeare, love becomes a tragic, all-consuming force that transcends family feuds and social expectations.

- **Family and Self-Love**: The theme of love within families is explored in novels like *King Lear*, where the King's relationships with his daughters, based on misplaced love and trust, lead to betrayal and tragedy. In the Victorian era, novels like *Pride and Prejudice* by Jane Austen examine familial love and the societal expectations of marriage, while also highlighting individual self-love and personal growth.
- **Modern Depictions**: In the 20th century, love continues to be explored, but with a focus on its darker, more complex sides. Authors like Virginia Woolf (*Mrs. Dalloway*) and Ian McEwan (*Atonement*) explore love as a force of both connection and alienation. In postmodern literature, love may be dissected as a social construct or examined in the context of cultural and historical changes, as seen in works by *Jeanette Winterson* (*Written on the Body*).

3. The Individual vs. Society

This recurring theme deals with the tension between personal desires, freedoms, and societal expectations or norms. The struggle between individualism and conformity, autonomy and control, runs throughout English literature, often reflecting the social, political, and cultural conflicts of the time.

- **Early Works**: In *Beowulf*, the hero's desire to achieve personal glory and honor sometimes conflicts with the responsibilities he has toward his people. This tension between the individual and the collective is also seen in medieval literature, where the hero must often make choices that balance personal ambition with loyalty to society.

- **In Shakespeare**: The theme is strongly evident in *Hamlet*, where Hamlet's internal conflict between personal desire for revenge and the duties expected of him as a prince creates a tragic outcome. Similarly, *The Merchant of Venice* explores the individual's pursuit of justice in the context of social norms and religious differences.

- **The Victorian Era**: This theme reaches its peak in the 19th century, where the conflict between the individual's desires and the expectations of society is central in novels like *Jane Eyre* by Charlotte Brontë, where the protagonist fights for personal freedom, and *Great Expectations* by Charles Dickens, where Pip's desire to rise above his social class causes tension with his humble origins.

- **Modern and Contemporary Literature**: In the 20th and 21st centuries, the theme of individual versus society becomes more nuanced, particularly in dystopian works like George Orwell's *1984*, where the individual's autonomy is entirely crushed by a totalitarian regime. In postmodern works, this theme is often explored through fragmentation and non-traditional narratives, as in Thomas Pynchon's *The Crying of Lot 49*.

4. The Corruption of Power

The theme of power and its corrupting influence has been explored in numerous English literary works, particularly those that address political and social structures. Characters who gain power often become morally compromised, revealing the dangers of unchecked authority.

- **Shakespearean Tragedies**: Power and its abuse are central themes in works like *Macbeth* and *Julius Caesar*. In *Macbeth*, the protagonist's rise to power through murder leads to his eventual downfall, highlighting the corrupting influence of ambition. In *Julius Caesar*, the assassination of the leader is motivated by the desire to preserve the Republic, but it ultimately leads to chaos and further corruption.

- **In the Victorian Era**: The theme of power and corruption is often explored through social class and institutions. Charles Dickens' *Bleak House* critiques the legal system's power, while in *Tess of the d'Urbervilles*, Thomas Hardy examines the corrupting effects of class and the control of women by patriarchal societal structures.

- **Modern Literature**: In works like George Orwell's *Animal Farm* and *Lord of the Flies* by William Golding, power is depicted as inherently corrupting, especially when unchallenged. Orwell critiques totalitarianism, while Golding examines the savagery that emerges in the absence of societal structure.

5. Death and Mortality

Death and mortality are universal themes that have been explored in English literature for centuries, reflecting both the inevitability of death and humanity's fear of the unknown.

- **In Medieval Literature**: In works like *The Canterbury Tales*, death is often a moral reckoning—characters are judged for their actions in life. The theme of death is also central in the *memento mori* tradition, reminding people of their mortality and the importance of leading virtuous lives.

- **Shakespearean Drama**: Shakespeare frequently explores death as both a literal and metaphorical end. In *Hamlet*, death is explored in the context of revenge, moral decay, and the afterlife. In *Macbeth*, the theme of death is intertwined with guilt, as the murder of Duncan leads to the protagonist's ultimate demise.
- **Modern Literature**: In 20th-century works like *The Death of Ivan Ilyich* by Leo Tolstoy (though not English, its influence on English writers is notable), death becomes a subject for existential reflection, exploring how one lives and what one leaves behind. In contemporary literature, authors often explore the complexity of death through fragmented narratives or in the context of medical technology and ethics.

6. Nature and the Sublime

Nature, particularly in its wild and uncontrollable form, is another key motif in English literature. The idea of the sublime—experiencing awe, terror, or beauty in nature—was central to the Romantic period, where poets like William Wordsworth, Samuel Taylor Coleridge, and John Keats depicted nature as a source of both spiritual and emotional power.

- **In Romanticism**: The poets of this period often celebrated nature as a pure, untainted force that provided a refuge from industrialization and urban life. For example, in Wordsworth's *Lines Composed a Few Miles Above Tintern Abbey*, nature is a place of healing and spiritual renewal.
- **The Victorian Era**: While the Victorians also found inspiration in nature, it was often in the context of social

and scientific progress. In *Middlemarch*, George Eliot explores how individuals engage with nature in relation to social and moral development.

- **Modern and Contemporary Works**: In the modern era, nature remains a powerful symbol of both beauty and destruction. Environmental literature, such as works by Rachel Carson (*Silent Spring*), addresses the impact of human activities on the natural world, while authors like J.R.R. Tolkien, in *The Lord of the Rings*, use nature as a central motif in their epic narratives.

The recurring themes and motifs in English literature reflect the changing concerns of society, culture, and human existence. From the heroic ideals of Old English literature to the complexities of postmodern narratives, themes like love, power, good and evil, death, and the individual vs. society persist, resonating with each new generation of readers. By analyzing these themes and motifs, readers can gain a deeper understanding of the diverse voices and experiences that shape the literary tradition, as well as the ways in which these works continue to resonate with modern readers.

CHAPTER XI

Literary Devices and Techniques

Literary devices and techniques are essential tools that writers use to convey their messages, evoke emotions, and add depth to their narratives. These devices shape the language of literature and help create meaning, atmosphere, and character development. Understanding these techniques enhances the reader's ability to interpret and appreciate a text, as they offer insight into the writer's intentions, creative choices, and the work's underlying themes. This chapter will introduce and explore some of the most common literary devices and techniques found in English literature.

1. Metaphor and Simile

Metaphor and **simile** are both comparisons that link one thing to another, but they do so in different ways.

- **Metaphor**: A metaphor directly compares two unlike things by stating one thing is another, creating a stronger, more immediate connection. This comparison suggests that the first object or concept embodies the qualities of the second.

Example: "Time is a thief."
Here, time is compared to a thief, suggesting that time steals moments or opportunities, even though time itself is not literally a thief.

- **Simile**: A simile compares two unlike things using the words "like" or "as." This makes the comparison less direct than a metaphor but still creates vivid imagery.

Example: "Her smile was as bright as the sun."
The smile is compared to the sun using "as," emphasizing its warmth and brightness.

Both devices are used to add layers of meaning and make the abstract more tangible, engaging the reader's imagination.

2. Allegory

An **allegory** is a narrative in which characters, events, or settings represent abstract ideas, moral qualities, or political concepts. Allegories often teach a lesson or convey a deeper message.

- **Example**: *Animal Farm* by George Orwell is a political allegory in which farm animals represent different social classes and political figures. Through the story, Orwell critiques the Russian Revolution and totalitarianism.

Allegories allow authors to make complex themes accessible by translating them into more understandable stories or symbols, often with clear moral or philosophical lessons.

3. Personification

Personification is a figure of speech in which non-human things are given human characteristics. This literary technique brings objects, animals, or ideas to life, making them more relatable and engaging.

- **Example**: "The wind whispered through the trees."
The wind is given the human ability to "whisper," creating a more vivid and emotional image of the natural

world.

Personification is often used to imbue nature, inanimate objects, or abstract ideas with emotion or agency, making them more vivid and creating a deeper connection between the reader and the narrative.

4. Irony

Irony involves a discrepancy between what is expected and what actually happens. There are several types of irony, each with its own characteristics:

- **Verbal Irony**: This occurs when a speaker says one thing but means the opposite, often with a tone of sarcasm.

  Example: "What a beautiful day!" (said during a storm)

- **Situational Irony**: This occurs when there is a stark contrast between what is expected to happen and what actually occurs.

  Example: A fire station burns down. One would expect a fire station to be immune to fire, making the event ironic.

- **Dramatic Irony**: This occurs when the audience knows something that the characters do not, creating tension or humor.

  Example: In *Romeo and Juliet*, the audience knows Juliet is not truly dead, but Romeo believes she is, leading to tragic consequences.

Irony highlights contradictions in life, often creating humor, suspense, or a deeper understanding of human nature.

5. Foreshadowing

Foreshadowing is a literary device in which the author hints at events or outcomes that will happen later in the narrative. It builds anticipation and prepares the reader for future developments, often creating suspense or a sense of inevitability.

- **Example**: In *Macbeth*, the witches' prophecy foreshadows Macbeth's rise to power and his eventual downfall. The ominous tone of their predictions sets the stage for the tragic events that unfold.

Foreshadowing can be subtle, hidden in small details or symbols, or more explicit, serving as a clear warning of what is to come.

6. Symbolism

Symbolism is the use of symbols—objects, characters, or events—that represent something beyond their literal meaning. A symbol is something that stands for an idea, quality, or concept, often adding layers of depth and meaning to a story.

- **Example**: In *The Great Gatsby*, the green light across the bay symbolizes Gatsby's unattainable dreams and his longing for the past.

Symbols can evoke emotions and themes that resonate with the reader, adding richness and complexity to the work.

7. Alliteration and Assonance

Both **alliteration** and **assonance** are sound devices that enhance the rhythm and musicality of a text, making it more engaging and memorable.

- **Alliteration** is the repetition of the same consonant sound at the beginning of words in close proximity.

  Example: "Peter Piper picked a peck of pickled peppers."

- **Assonance** is the repetition of vowel sounds within nearby words, creating a kind of internal rhyme.

  Example: "Hear the mellow wedding bells."

Both devices are often used in poetry and prose to create a pleasing auditory effect, heightening the mood or tone of the piece.

8. Flashback

A **flashback** is a narrative technique in which the author interrupts the chronological sequence of events to provide information about an earlier time. Flashbacks provide background or context, often revealing important events that shape the characters or plot.

- **Example:** In *The Great Gatsby*, Nick Carraway often uses flashbacks to recount events that led to the novel's present-day scenario, offering insight into Gatsby's past and motivations.

Flashbacks help to deepen characters' histories and motivations, enriching the storyline with additional layers of meaning and context.

9. Anagnorisis and Peripeteia

Anagnorisis refers to the moment in a play or story when a character makes a critical discovery, usually related to their identity or the truth of their situation. **Peripeteia**, on the other hand, is a sudden reversal of fortune or change in circumstances that leads to the climax of the story.

- **Example**: In *Oedipus Rex* by Sophocles, Oedipus experiences both anagnorisis (the realization that he has killed his father and married his mother) and peripeteia (the shift from his kingship to his tragic downfall).

These two devices are central to classical tragedy, contributing to the dramatic structure and emotional impact of the narrative.

10. Paradox

A **paradox** is a statement or situation that appears contradictory but may reveal an underlying truth. Paradoxes challenge readers to think critically about concepts that seem to defy logic or common sense.

- **Example**: "Less is more."
  The phrase suggests that simplicity can be more powerful or effective than excess, despite appearing contradictory.

Paradoxes force the reader to confront the complexity of human experience, where opposites can coexist and yield deeper insights.

11. Motif

A **motif** is a recurring element, such as a theme, symbol, or idea, that appears throughout a literary work. Motifs help to develop the work's themes and can reinforce its central messages.

- **Example**: The motif of *light and darkness* appears throughout *Romeo and Juliet*, representing love and fate. The characters often speak of light as a symbol of love and hope, while darkness symbolizes the obstacles and tragedy they face.

Motifs help create cohesion in a work by linking various parts of the narrative and emphasizing important themes or messages.

12. Tone and Mood

Tone refers to the writer's attitude toward the subject or audience, while **mood** is the atmosphere or emotional feeling that the text evokes in the reader.

- **Tone** can be serious, humorous, sarcastic, or ironic, and it reflects the writer's point of view.

Example: The tone of *Pride and Prejudice* is witty and ironic, with Austen using sharp humor to comment on societal norms.

- **Mood** is the emotional response the author seeks to evoke in the reader, such as joy, sadness, fear, or tension.

Example: The mood of *Wuthering Heights* is dark and brooding, reflecting the tumultuous relationships and tragic events that unfold in the novel.

Understanding tone and mood helps readers to connect more deeply with the emotional undercurrents of a work and its thematic content.

Literary devices and techniques are fundamental to understanding and appreciating the complexities of English literature. Writers use these tools to craft stories that resonate with readers on an emotional and intellectual level. By recognizing and analyzing these devices, readers can gain a deeper insight into how language functions within literature, enhancing their experience and interpretation of texts. From the subtle use of symbolism to the dramatic effect of irony, these techniques shape not only the narrative structure but also the themes and meanings embedded in a work.

75

CHAPTER XII

Conclusion: The Impact of English Literature

English literature, spanning over centuries, has had an undeniable influence on shaping the intellectual, cultural, and social fabric of societies around the world. From the ancient works of Beowulf to contemporary novels and poetry, literature has served as a mirror of human experience, offering insight into our deepest emotions, societal norms, historical contexts, and personal identities. In this conclusion, we will explore the enduring impact of English literature, focusing on its role in shaping society, culture, and individual perspectives.

1. Reflecting Society and Culture

One of the most powerful functions of English literature is its ability to reflect the social and cultural dynamics of its time. Literary works act as a lens through which we can examine historical events, social structures, and cultural movements. Whether it's Shakespeare's exploration of human nature, Charles Dickens' critique of Victorian society, or Toni Morrison's examination of race and identity in America, literature has long provided commentary on the world in which it was created.

- **Example:** In *The Great Gatsby*, F. Scott Fitzgerald critiques the American Dream, exploring themes of wealth, class, and disillusionment in the context of 1920s America. The novel not only highlights the era's materialism and excess but also serves as a cautionary tale about the pursuit of unattainable ideals.

- **Example**: In *Pride and Prejudice*, Jane Austen uses the relationships and social mobility of her characters to critique the class system and gender roles of Regency England, making her work both a social commentary and a timeless exploration of human nature.

English literature provides a historical record, helping readers gain a deeper understanding of the values, struggles, and triumphs of different cultures throughout time. It allows individuals to connect with and reflect on the experiences of others, fostering empathy, understanding, and social change.

2. Shaping Identity and Human Experience

Literature offers a space for individuals to explore their own identity, both personally and as part of a larger community. Through the characters, themes, and narratives presented in literary works, readers often find reflections of their own experiences, struggles, and dreams. English literature allows individuals to grapple with universal themes such as love, loss, identity, morality, and freedom. The process of engaging with these ideas and characters can lead to self-discovery, a deepened sense of empathy, and a better understanding of one's place in the world.

- **Example**: James Baldwin's *Giovanni's Room* explores themes of sexual identity, self-acceptance, and alienation, providing an introspective look at the complexities of personal identity. Baldwin's work resonates with readers who are navigating their own experiences of self-discovery and societal expectations.

- **Example**: In *Beloved*, Toni Morrison delves into the trauma of slavery and its lasting effects on both individual and collective memory. The novel not only reflects the painful history of African Americans but also examines the psychological and emotional scars of slavery, offering readers an opportunity to reflect on the complex dynamics of race and history.

Through the personal journeys of characters, English literature provides a rich tapestry of human experiences, allowing readers to see themselves in the stories, expand their perspectives, and explore new ways of thinking about their identity and the world around them.

3. Inspiring Change and Social Justice

English literature has often played a crucial role in advocating for social justice, challenging societal norms, and inspiring political and cultural change. Writers have used their works to expose injustices, question authority, and raise awareness about the plight of marginalized communities. Literature serves as both a tool for reflection and a catalyst for action, motivating readers to question the status quo and imagine new possibilities for a more just and equitable world.

- **Example**: Harriet Beecher Stowe's *Uncle Tom's Cabin* was instrumental in shaping public opinion about slavery in the United States, helping to galvanize the abolitionist movement. Stowe's vivid portrayal of the human suffering caused by slavery played a significant role in fostering empathy and pushing for political change.
- **Example**: In *1984*, George Orwell uses dystopian fiction to critique totalitarianism and government surveillance.

His exploration of the mechanisms of control and oppression has continued to resonate with readers concerned about the dangers of unchecked political power, making the novel a timeless warning about the need for vigilance and resistance.

Through their exploration of social issues, authors have not only provided a means for cultural critique but have also helped inspire movements for change, whether through the abolition of slavery, the advancement of civil rights, or the push for gender equality. English literature empowers readers to imagine a better world and challenges them to take action in shaping it.

4. Expanding the Boundaries of Human Imagination

Literature, especially English literature, plays an essential role in expanding the boundaries of human imagination. Writers have the ability to transport readers to different times, places, and realities, allowing them to experience worlds beyond their own. Through storytelling, writers explore philosophical questions, alternative realities, and moral dilemmas, creating rich spaces for creative thought and intellectual exploration. Whether through poetry, plays, or novels, literature allows us to engage with complex ideas in an imaginative way.

- **Example:** J.R.R. Tolkien's *The Lord of the Rings* creates an expansive fantasy world filled with rich histories, cultures, and languages. The series challenges readers to think about power, good vs. evil, friendship, and heroism in profound ways, all while immersing them in an imaginative universe.
- **Example:** Virginia Woolf's *Mrs. Dalloway* explores consciousness, memory, and identity in ways that push

the boundaries of narrative structure and style. Her modernist techniques offer readers new ways of understanding the passage of time and the complexity of individual experience.

Through its focus on the fantastical and the philosophical, literature allows readers to transcend the limitations of the immediate and the everyday, inviting them into a space where imagination can flourish.

5. Fostering Cross-Cultural Connections

English literature, as a global medium, fosters cross-cultural connections and promotes the exchange of ideas. Through the translation of works from other languages or the incorporation of diverse voices within English-language literature, readers gain access to new perspectives on the human condition. Writers from various parts of the world contribute to the ever-expanding body of English literature, creating a dialogue between cultures that enriches the literary tradition and broadens readers' horizons.

- **Example**: Chinua Achebe's *Things Fall Apart* offers a powerful exploration of colonialism, tradition, and change in Igbo society. Achebe's work bridges the gap between African literature and English literary traditions, contributing to a more global understanding of the impacts of European imperialism.
- **Example**: Salman Rushdie's *Midnight's Children* weaves together the history and culture of postcolonial India, offering a narrative that spans both personal and national struggles, providing readers from different backgrounds with a window into the complexity of identity in a postcolonial world.

Through these intercultural exchanges, English literature not only enriches the readers' understanding of the world but also highlights the shared humanity that connects us all.

6. A Timeless Legacy

The impact of English literature is vast and profound. Its ability to reflect society, shape identities, inspire social change, expand imagination, and foster cultural understanding makes it an essential part of human history and civilization. Literature offers a timeless record of human experience, capturing the complexities of emotion, thought, and social existence. From the classics to contemporary works, English literature will continue to influence generations, provoke thought, and inspire action.

As we reflect on the enduring power of English literature, we recognize that it is not just a collection of written works but a living, evolving tradition that reflects the ever-changing nature of human life. Writers will continue to shape and challenge our understanding of the world, and readers will find new meaning in the pages of literature for generations to come.

In the end, the study and enjoyment of English literature is not just an academic pursuit but a gateway to deeper human understanding, personal growth, and a greater appreciation of the diversity and complexity of the world around us.

www.ingramcontent.com/pod-product-compliance
Lightning Source LLC
Chambersburg PA
CBHW061438160726
47995CB00003B/941